BoE 3969

HANS-GÜNTER HEUMANN
Children's Pop Piano

POPPIGE SPIELSTÜCKE
IN LEICHTER FASSUNG
FÜR KLAVIER/KEYBOARD

POP SETTINGS IN EASY
SETTINGS FOR PIANO/KEYBOARD

Heft 2 / Book 2

INHALT/INDEX

		Seite/Page
①	**Amazing Grace** (Trad.)	2
②	**Yesterday** (John Lennon/Paul McCartney)	4
③	**Aloha Oë** (Queen Liliuokalani)	6
④	**Good Night, Ladies** (Trad.)	8
⑤	**Swingin' Blue**	9
⑥	**Guantanamera** (Trad.)	10
⑦	**Rock Feeling**	12
⑧	**Honky Tonk Piano**	14
⑨	**Rock a Bit**	16
⑩	**Chattanooga Choo Choo** (Harry Warren/Mack Gordon)	18
⑪	**What Shall We Do with the Drunken Sailor** (Trad.)	20
⑫	**Alexander's Ragtime Band** (Irving Berlin)	22

© Copyright MCMLXXXVII by Bosworth GmbH., Berlin

BOSWORTH EDITION

Amazing Grace

Traditional
Arr.: Hans-Günter Heumann

Allegro e cantabile M.M. ♪ = 144-152

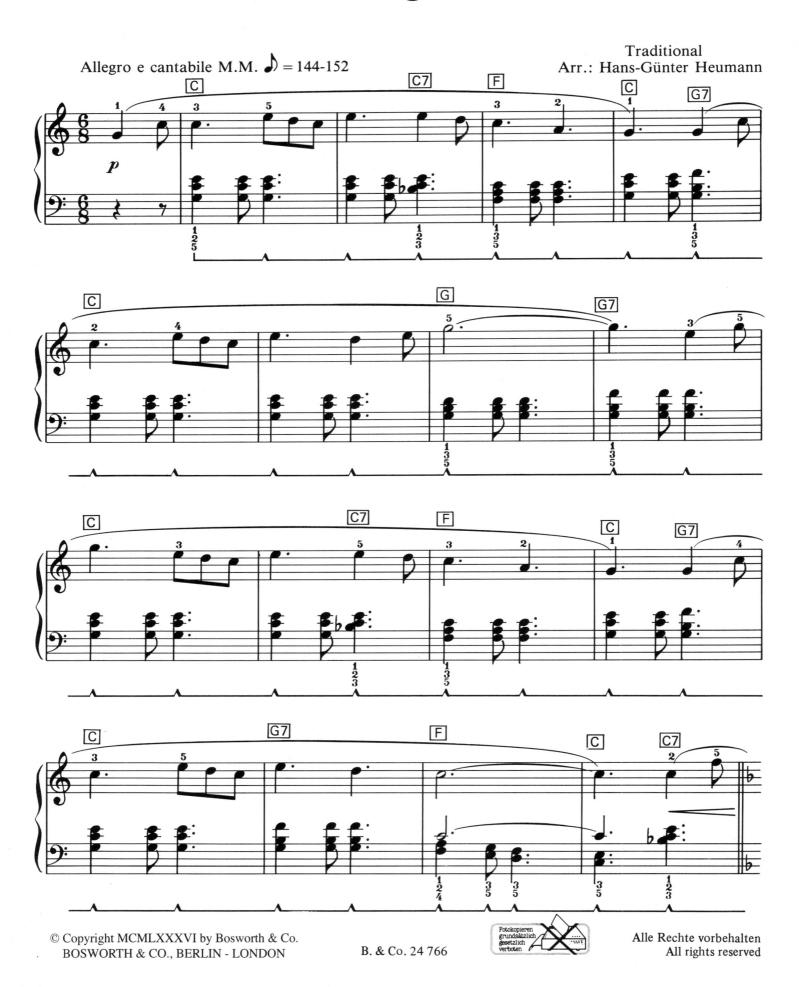

Yesterday

Words & Music by John Lennon & Paul McCartney
Arr.: Hans-Günter Heumann

© Copyright 1965 by NORTHERN SONG LIMITED
used by permission of Music Sales Limited.
International Copyright Secured.

Alle Rechte vorbehalten
All rights reserved

Aloha Oë

Music by Liliuokalani
Arr.: Hans-Günter Heumann

Good Night, Ladies

Traditional
Arr.: Hans-Günter Heumann

Swingin' Blue

Hans-Günter Heumann

Guantanamera

Traditional
Arr.: Hans-Günter Heumann

Rock Feeling

Honky Tonk Piano

Hans-Günter Heumann

Rock a Bit

Hans-Günter Heumann

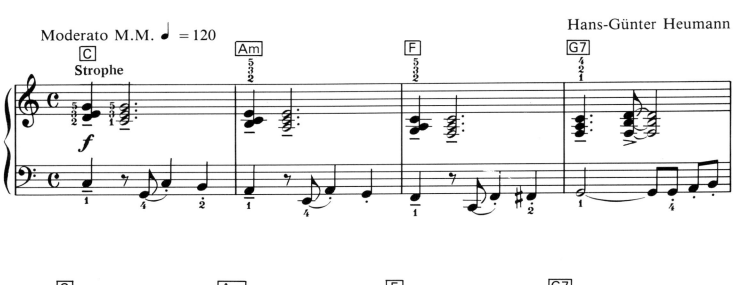

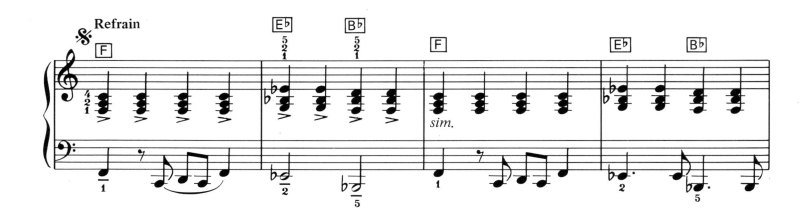
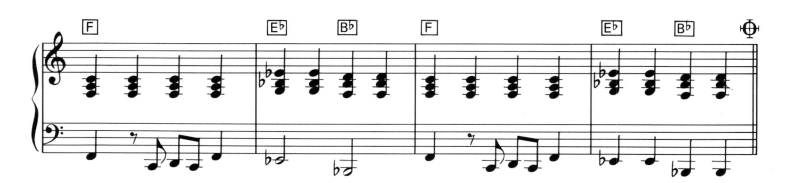

© Copyright MCMLXXXVI by Bosworth & Co.
BOSWORTH & CO., BERLIN - LONDON

Alle Rechte vorbehalten
All rights reserved

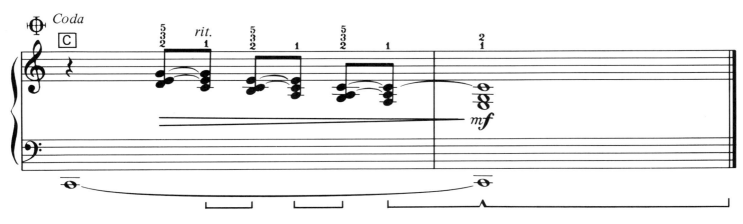

Chattanooga Choo Choo

Music by Harry Warren
Arr.: Hans-Günter Heumann

©1941 EMI Catalogue Partnership/EMI Feist Catalog Inc. USA
Worldwide print rights controlled by Warner Bros. Publications Inc./IMP Ltd.
Reproduced by permission of IMP Ltd.

Alle Rechte vorbehalten
All rights reserved

What Shall We Do with the Drunken Sailor

Alexander's Ragtime Band

Music by Irving Berlin
Arr.: Hans-Günter Heumann

© Copyright MCMXI by Irving Berlin
© Copyright renewed MCMXXXVIII by Irving Berlin
Für Deutschland, Österreich, Ungarn, C.S.S.R. Polen, Finnland, Skandinavien, Lettland, Estland, Holland und die deutsche Schweiz:
BOSWORTH & CO., BERLIN - LONDON

Alle Rechte vorbehalten
All rights reserved

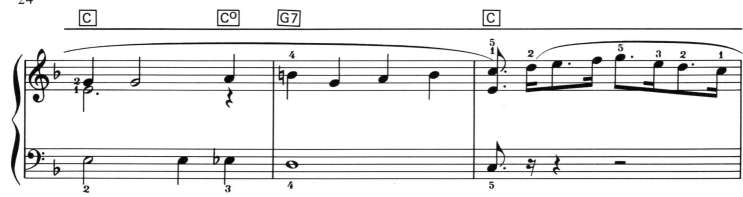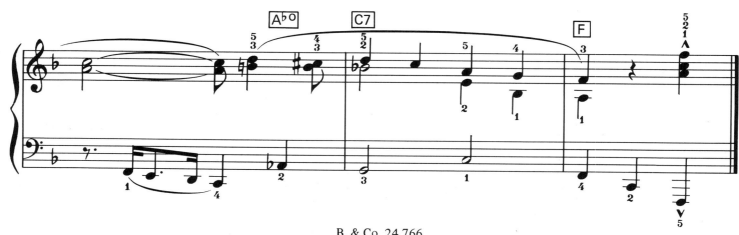